Understanding AI:

A Beginner's Guide

Introduction

- What is AI? (A clear, engaging definition)

- Why understanding AI matters in today's world

- The purpose of this eBook: demystifying AI for everyone

Chapter 1: The History of AI

- The origin of AI and early developments

- Key milestones in AI history (e.g., Turing test, neural networks)

- AI in pop culture vs. reality

Chapter 2: How AI Works

- Basics of machine learning, neural networks, and algorithms

- The role of data in AI

- Types of AI: narrow, general, and superintelligence

Chapter 3: AI in Everyday Life

- Examples of AI you already use (smartphones, recommendations, etc.)

- The impact of AI on various industries (healthcare, education, etc.)

- The role of AI in personalization

Chapter 4: Ethics and Challenges

- Concerns about bias, privacy, and transparency

- Debunking common myths and fears about AI

- The balance between innovation and ethical use

Chapter 5: The Future of AI

- Trends and advancements to watch for

- Potential societal changes AI could bring

- The importance of responsible development

Chapter 6: How to Interact with AI

- Tips for using AI tools responsibly

- Teaching children and others about AI

- The importance of respect in human-AI collaboration (a nod to your teaching philosophy)

Conclusion

- Recap of key takeaways

- Encouragement for continued learning about AI

- Resources for deeper exploration

Introduction: So, What's the Deal with AI Anyway?

Imagine this: you're scrolling through your favorite app, and it recommends a pair of socks that match your personality. "How does it *know* me so well?" you think, half-flattered, half-creeped out. Welcome to the world of Artificial Intelligence—or, as I like to call it, the brainiac behind your playlists, your autocorrect fails, and yes, those oddly specific sock ads.

AI has been making waves lately, showing up everywhere from your smart fridge to your friend's overly chatty chatbot. But if you've ever found yourself nodding along to conversations about AI, secretly wondering if "machine learning" is some kind of workout for robots, you're not alone. Trust me, no one was born understanding neural networks. (If they were, I'm concerned.)

The truth is, AI isn't some mysterious wizard hiding behind a curtain, nor is it a sci-fi villain plotting world domination. It's a tool—albeit a pretty cool and complex one—that's reshaping the way we live, work, and even think. And here's the kicker: you don't have to be a tech genius to get it.

This Book is your backstage pass to the world of AI. I'll break down the jargon, bust some myths, and maybe even make you laugh along the way. (Yes, robots can be funny—or at least try. Just wait until we get to the "dad joke generator" part.)

Whether you're here out of curiosity, a desire to impress your friends, or because you clicked on the wrong link and are too polite to leave, you're in the right place. By the time we're done, you'll not only *understand* AI, but you might just feel a little smarter than the algorithms running your Netflix queue.

So, grab a cup of coffee—or let your smart coffee maker brew it for you—and let's dive into the fascinating, sometimes weird, always exciting world of AI. Who knows? By the end, you might even teach *it* a thing or two.

Chapter 1: The History of AI (From Sci-Fi Dreams to Reality)

Let's take a stroll down memory lane—the story of Artificial Intelligence didn't start with Alexa correcting your weather guess or that time Siri hilariously misunderstood you. It goes way back, long before computers were even a thing. Back when the idea of intelligent machines was pure science fiction—or maybe just wishful thinking.

The Ancient AI Dreamers

Humans have been fantasizing about creating intelligent beings for centuries. Ancient myths featured mechanical servants, like Talos, the bronze giant of Greek mythology, who guarded Crete (basically the world's first bouncer). These stories weren't *exactly* AI, but they hinted at our obsession with building something smarter than your average mortal.

Fast forward to the 13th century: Roger Bacon, an English philosopher, mused about machines that could perform tasks for humans. Spoiler alert: his plans didn't pan out.

The Spark of Genius: 20th-Century Foundations

The real action started in the mid-20th century when technology finally caught up with our imagination. In 1950, computer science pioneer Alan Turing wrote a groundbreaking paper titled *"Computing Machinery and Intelligence."* He asked the big question: "Can machines think?" (Cue dramatic music.)

This was the same guy who cracked codes during World War II and basically invented the computer as we know it. He also developed the "Turing Test," a way to measure if an AI is convincing enough to pass as human in conversation. So, if you've ever been freaked out by a chatbot being *too* good, blame Turing.

The 1950s-1970s: AI Takes Baby Steps

In 1956, a group of brainy dudes at Dartmouth College coined the term "Artificial Intelligence." The goal? To make machines capable of human-like reasoning. Lofty, right? But they didn't get robots solving crimes or writing sonnets overnight. Instead, they spent years teaching computers to solve puzzles and play games like chess.

By the 1970s, AI started facing what historians call its "winter phase." Turns out, building human-level intelligence is...hard. Funding dried up, and researchers stopped daydreaming about robot assistants and focused on simpler goals, like making computers not crash every five minutes.

The AI Comeback Kid: 1980s to Now

AI bounced back in the 1980s when computers got faster and cheaper. Expert systems (programs designed to simulate decision-making) took off, and industries like medicine started noticing AI could be useful for diagnosing diseases. By the 2000s, AI had crept into everyday life—Google, Amazon, and Apple were quietly turning search engines and voice assistants into household staples.

Then came the Big Bang moment: neural networks. Inspired by the way human brains work (minus the coffee addiction), these systems taught machines how to *learn* instead of just following rigid instructions. Suddenly, AI wasn't just calculating—it was recognizing faces, understanding speech, and recommending you the perfect cat video at 2 a.m.

Pop Culture vs. Reality: Hollywood's Love Affair with AI

Meanwhile, movies like *2001: A Space Odyssey* and *The Terminator* turned AI into either a supervillain or a tragic genius. In real life, AI wasn't plotting world domination—it was more concerned with learning to beat humans at Jeopardy! (*Thanks, Watson.*)

Hollywood made AI cool, but it also gave us a few myths to bust. Like, no, AI isn't self-aware, and your Roomba isn't secretly judging your housekeeping skills.

Why This History Matters

Understanding where AI comes from helps us appreciate where it's going. It's easy to see today's AI as just a flashy gadget, but it's the result of decades (even centuries) of human curiosity, innovation, and, let's be honest, a fair bit of trial and error.

So, as you scroll through the rest of this Book, remember: AI isn't magic. It's human ingenuity coded into zeros and ones. And that's what makes it both fascinating and a little bit funny—it's the brainchild of people like you and me who dared to ask, "What if?"

Chapter 2: How AI Works (No Tech Degree Required)

Alright, so now that we've taken a walk through AI's history, it's time to crack open the hood and figure out what's going on inside. But don't worry—you won't need a PhD in computer science to follow along. Think of this chapter as your AI cheat sheet, where we simplify the complex and make you sound like the smartest person in the room (without the jargon).

AI 101: What's the Big Idea?

At its core, Artificial Intelligence is about teaching machines to think—or at least fake it well enough to impress us. Instead of coding every single rule (like, "If A happens, do B"), AI uses *data* to learn patterns, make predictions, and solve problems.

Picture a toddler learning to recognize a dog. You don't give them a dictionary definition of "dog." You just point and say, "That's a dog." Show them enough examples, and they'll figure out the difference between a Chihuahua and a horse (hopefully). AI works the same way—it learns by example.

The Building Blocks of AI

Let's break it down into digestible pieces:

1. **Algorithms: The Recipe for AI**

   An algorithm is just a fancy word for a set of instructions. It's like a recipe for baking a cake, except instead of flour and eggs, you're working with data and math. AI algorithms analyze data to figure out patterns and make decisions—kind of like a detective piecing together clues.

2. **Machine Learning: The Magic Sauce**

   Machine learning is a type of AI where computers don't just follow instructions—they *learn* from experience. Feed them enough data (like millions of pictures of cats), and they'll start recognizing patterns (like, "Oh, cats usually have pointy ears and judgmental stares").

   a. **Supervised Learning:** Think of it like training a dog. You give the computer examples with clear answers ("This is a cat, this is not"), and it learns to predict new cases.

b. **Unsupervised Learning:** No training wheels here. The computer looks for patterns on its own, like finding groups of similar data (e.g., "These customers all love tacos").

c. **Reinforcement Learning:** This is trial and error on steroids. The AI learns by doing, getting rewards for good outcomes (like winning a game) and penalties for bad ones (like crashing a virtual car).

3. **Neural Networks: AI's Brain-Inspired Tech**

Neural networks mimic the way human brains work—minus the daydreaming and caffeine dependency. They're made up of layers of "neurons" that process information, passing it along until they've figured something out. This is how AI can do wild stuff like recognize faces or understand speech.

Data: The Fuel for AI

If AI is the engine, data is the fuel. Tons of it. AI thrives on examples—millions, if not billions, of them. Whether it's photos, text, or numbers, the more data AI gets, the better it becomes.

But here's the kicker: not all data is good data. If you feed an AI biased or incomplete information, it'll make biased or incomplete decisions. It's like trying to learn how to cook using only microwave meal instructions—you'll get...mixed results.

AI in Action: An Example

Let's say you want to build an AI to recommend movies. Here's how it might work:

1. **Input Data:** Feed it info about movies (genre, director, ratings) and user preferences.

2. **Training:** The AI analyzes past patterns, like "People who loved *Star Wars* also loved *The Mandalorian*."

3. **Prediction:** When you log in, it suggests new titles based on your taste—hopefully without judgment about your secret love for rom-coms.

The Limitations of AI (Yes, It's Not Perfect)

Before we crown AI the king of intelligence, let's talk about its limits. AI isn't "smart" in the human sense—it doesn't understand context, emotions, or nuance. It's great at doing specific tasks but completely clueless outside its training. (Ask your virtual assistant to tell a joke and you'll see what I mean.)

And then there's the infamous "garbage in, garbage out" problem. If you feed AI bad data, it'll give you bad results. Think of it like trusting a random stranger to bake your wedding cake—they might nail it, or they might hand you a pile of burnt dough.

Why This Matters

Understanding how AI works isn't just for tech nerds. It's for anyone who uses a smartphone, shops online, or has ever yelled at a GPS for getting them lost. Knowing the basics helps you spot AI's strengths, call out its flaws, and use it to your advantage—whether that's planning your day or writing an eBook like this one.

So, now that you know *how* AI works, it's time to explore where it's showing up in your everyday life. Spoiler alert: it's everywhere.

Chapter 3: AI in Everyday Life (Yes, It's Everywhere)

Let's face it: AI has quietly taken over the world—not in a sci-fi, robot-uprising kind of way, but in a much sneakier, more helpful way. It's woven into your day from the moment your alarm rings (set by AI, of course) to the time you fall asleep streaming your favorite show.

If you think AI is just for techies, think again. Whether you're asking your phone for directions, shopping online, or binge-watching a crime drama that *definitely* wasn't your idea (thanks, Netflix), AI is there, working its magic behind the scenes.

AI in Your Pocket: Smartphones

Your smartphone is basically a pocket-sized AI wizard. From facial recognition to autocomplete, AI is the reason your device feels like it knows you better than you know yourself.

- **Voice Assistants:** Whether it's Siri, Alexa, or Google Assistant, these AI-powered helpers can answer your questions, set reminders, or tell you terrible jokes. (Seriously, someone teach them better punchlines.)

- **Autocorrect and Predictive Text:** AI learns your typing habits and tries to guess your next word. Sure, sometimes it gets it hilariously wrong, but hey, nobody's perfect.

- **Photo Sorting:** Remember when organizing your photo albums was a chore? Now AI can recognize faces, locations, and even objects in your pictures, making it easier to find that one selfie you took on vacation.

AI in Your Home: Smart Gadgets

From smart thermostats to robot vacuums, AI has made its way into our homes, making life a little easier (and lazier).

- **Smart Speakers:** These AI-powered devices can play music, control your lights, and even order pizza—all without you lifting a finger. Just try not to argue with them; they're sensitive.

- **Robot Vacuums:** Sure, they bump into walls like drunk toddlers, but they eventually figure out how to clean your floors.

- **Smart Appliances:** AI-powered fridges can suggest recipes based on what's inside, while smart ovens can cook your food to perfection. (No more blaming the oven for burnt cookies.)

AI at Work: Behind the Scenes of Business

AI isn't just for consumers—it's transforming industries, too. Companies use AI to analyze data, automate tasks, and even make hiring decisions.

- **Customer Service Chatbots:** Those "live chats" you see on websites? Surprise, most of them are AI. They're great for answering basic questions but don't expect them to understand your life story.

- **Marketing:** Ever wondered how that ad for running shoes followed you across the internet? AI tracks your browsing habits to deliver eerily specific ads.

- **Healthcare:** AI is helping doctors diagnose diseases, analyze scans, and even predict patient outcomes. It's like having a super-smart medical assistant that never takes a coffee break.

AI in Entertainment: Keeping You Hooked

Whether you're streaming, gaming, or scrolling, AI is working overtime to keep you entertained.

- **Streaming Services:** Netflix, Hulu, and Spotify use AI to recommend shows, movies, and music based on your preferences. (Though sometimes you have to wonder, "Why does it think I'd like this?")

- **Video Games:** AI controls non-player characters (NPCs), making them smarter and more realistic. It's also used to create adaptive difficulty levels, so you're always challenged but not frustrated.

- **Social Media:** AI decides what posts to show you, which ads to display, and which videos you absolutely must see at 3 a.m.

AI in the Wild: Surprising Uses

AI isn't just limited to tech and business—it's popping up in some unexpected places:

- **Agriculture:** Farmers use AI to monitor crops, predict weather patterns, and optimize irrigation. It's like having a high-tech scarecrow.

- **Art and Creativity:** AI can create paintings, write poems, and compose music. It's not Beethoven, but it's getting there.

- **Conservation:** AI-powered drones help track endangered species and monitor deforestation, proving that technology can save the planet (or at least try).

Why This Matters

Knowing how AI is already a part of your life helps you appreciate its benefits—and spot its flaws. The next time you ask Siri to set an alarm or let Netflix decide your Friday night plans, you'll understand the smarts (and the quirks) behind it.

And now that we've explored AI in the present, it's time to look ahead. What does the future hold for AI? Let's dive into Chapter 4 and find out.

Chapter 4: The Future of AI (Bold Predictions & Wild Possibilities)

AI today feels like magic, but the truth is, we're just scratching the surface. From flying cars to robot best friends, the future of AI has endless possibilities—and a few curveballs. Some of these ideas might seem straight out of science fiction, but hey, people once thought Wi-Fi was wizardry too.

Let's peek into the crystal ball and explore where AI is heading. Spoiler alert: it's going to get weirder, cooler, and possibly a little unsettling.

AI That Feels Human: Emotional Intelligence

Imagine an AI that doesn't just understand *what* you're saying but *how* you're feeling. Emotional AI is already in the works, and it's designed to read your tone, facial expressions, and even your text messages to gauge your mood.

- **Applications:**
    - Virtual therapists that offer real-time emotional support.
    - Customer service bots that don't sound like, well, robots.
    - AI companions for those late-night existential crises.

But here's the question: Do we really want a machine to know when we're hangry?

The Rise of Autonomous Everything

Self-driving cars are just the beginning. The future is filled with autonomous systems that will run errands, deliver goods, and even cook dinner.

- **Transportation:** Autonomous vehicles might become the norm, from driverless taxis to AI-controlled delivery drones. Say goodbye to road rage (but maybe hello to drone traffic jams).

- **Homes:** Imagine a fully automated house that adjusts the temperature, locks the doors, and even folds your laundry— all while you binge-watch your favorite show.

- **Workplaces:** Robots handling tedious tasks? Yes, please. AI could make workplaces more efficient, freeing humans to focus on creative and strategic work.

Of course, with all this autonomy comes one big question: what happens if the system breaks down? (Let's hope the tech support AI is ready.)

AI in Medicine: Living Longer, Living Smarter

AI is already making waves in healthcare, but the future promises even greater advancements:

- **Precision Medicine:** AI could analyze your DNA and create personalized treatment plans.

- **Disease Prediction:** Imagine knowing you're at risk for a health issue years before symptoms appear.

- **Robotic Surgeons:** Robots already assist in surgeries, but fully autonomous AI surgeons? That's coming too.

The idea of a robot holding a scalpel might sound terrifying, but studies suggest they'll make fewer mistakes than humans. (Still, it's hard not to picture it saying, "Oops.")

Supercharged Creativity: Art, Music, and Beyond

AI isn't just for logical tasks—it's flexing its creative muscles too. In the future, AI could:

- Write bestselling novels (watch out, human authors).

- Compose symphonies that rival Beethoven's.

- Design buildings, clothes, and even movies.

But here's the catch: Can a machine truly understand art? Or will it just copy what it's seen before? That debate is already heating up—and AI hasn't even written its first Oscar speech yet.

AI & Ethics: The Big Questions

As AI becomes more powerful, the ethical dilemmas grow too. Some of the big ones include:

- **Bias:** How do we ensure AI doesn't inherit human prejudices?

- **Privacy:** With AI collecting so much data, how do we protect our personal information?

- **Job Displacement:** What happens when machines take over more human jobs?

The good news? Humans still get the final say (for now). The challenge is building AI systems that align with our values—and figuring out what those values should be.

The Singularity: Sci-Fi or Reality?

Ah, the singularity—that mythical point when AI becomes so advanced it surpasses human intelligence. Some say it'll happen in the next few decades; others think it's a sci-fi fantasy.

If it does happen, will AI become our best friend, our overlord, or something in between? It's hard to say. But one thing's for sure: we'll need to be prepared, whether that means embracing AI as a partner or programming it to love cats as much as the internet does.

The Takeaway

The future of AI is equal parts exciting and uncertain. It has the potential to solve some of humanity's biggest challenges—but it also raises new questions about what it means to be human.

As we move forward, one thing is clear: AI isn't just shaping our world; it's becoming a part of it. And whether we're ready or not, the future is coming fast.